What did the box say?

Gathoni Njenga

What did the box say?

Gathoni Njenga

BOX

THINK

Don't be afraid
to think outside
the box

But what does that mean?

It means don't be afraid to try something new

Don't be afraid to change your views

Don't be
afraid to be

Sometimes it's in with the new and out with the old

Don't be afraid to be different

Don't be afraid to
"go it alone"
sometimes.

Be brave little one!

Be
creative

Be open to
new ideas

Be open to new people..

... new friends

.....new teachers

.... a new school

You'll never
know till you try

Certificate
You'll never know
till you think
Outside the box

THE END

ABOUT THE AUTHOR

Author and illustrator
Gathoni Njenga through
her Ostrich kids brand
seeks to educate and
inspire little boys and
girls all over the world.

Happy kids!

Make the world a happy place.
Here is to doing our part to help bring
joy to kids all over the world.

OSTRICH KIDS

www.ingramcontent.com/pod-product-compliance
Lightning Source LLC
Chambersburg PA
CBHW040940110726
48006CB00001B/215